# MYSTERIES, MIRACLES, & AMAZING STORIES

Curious Cats and How They Bless Our Lives

Inspired by Faith

Mysteries, Miracles, & Amazing Stories
©Product Concept Mfg., Inc.

Mysteries, Miracles, & Amazing Stories
ISBN 978-0-9835438-8-6

Published by Product Concept Mfg., Inc.
2175 N. Academy Circle #200, Colorado Springs, CO 80909

Sayings not having a credit listed are contributed by writers
for Product Concept Mfg., Inc. or in a rare case,
the author is unknown.

Written and Compiled by Patricia Mitchell
in association with Product Concept Mfg., Inc.

# MYSTERIES, MIRACLES, & AMAZING STORIES

Time spent with a cat is never wasted.
- Saying

These pages are filled with stories——some of them true and some of them based on real events. There are stories you may recognize, having heard or read them in the distant past...and others that, if you love cats, you will think to yourself, "Yes, it could have happened exactly this way."

There are stories to astonish you, amaze you, entertain you, warm your heart, and make you laugh. And each one comes with a reflection and quotations...something to ponder, if you're so inclined...because there's nothing a cat can do that doesn't somehow echo in our own lives and memories.

You can read this book cover to cover, or pick it up as a cat might...that is, whenever you feel like it. Open it anywhere and begin reading about cats behaving marvelously, strangely, mysteriously. You might wonder, "What if?"..."Could it have been?"..."Oh, something like that happened to me, too." Your favorite cat——the one in your lap...the one in your heart...the one at your door today or tomorrow——will know exactly what you mean.

# KITTENS IN HIGH PLACES

T he kitten came into our house—then vanished. We searched under our bed, inside closets, beneath the staircase, behind the sofa, and on top of shelves. Every time we passed a window, we scanned the yard, just in case she had scampered outside. In a matter of seconds, the mischievous ball of fur had outwitted both of her new two-legged friends, and we finally admitted we were bested.

"She didn't get out, I'm sure," my husband said. "I can't imagine how", I agreed. "I guess she'll come out when she's ready." Certainly this wasn't the homecoming I had planned for her, and I spent the rest of the day on the lookout for a sweet fuzzy creature with snowy vest and silver coat to appear. Whatever I did, I also listened for her soft, melodic meow to drift out from somewhere we had forgotten to look.

By nighttime, I was exhausted, and left my husband to the evening news while I went upstairs to bed. I couldn't get my mind off the kitten. I felt we had let her down by allowing her to dart into a strange house and navigate for herself these unfamiliar surroundings. I imagined myself in her place—frightened, alone, disoriented—and I was heartsick. I showered, slipped on my PJs, crawled onto bed, stretched out and put my head on the pillow. That's when I spied the telltale lump.

Inspired by a picture in a home décor magazine, I had draped long ivory swags over a hook high on the wall above our bed. The fabric reached the floor on both sides of our bed, and could easily accommodate a kitten using them to rappel up to the top. Immediately, I stood up on the bed to peer inside the "lumpy" fold turned cradle. I was greeted by two tiny blue eyes looking into mine. "Why were you making such a fuss?" those eyes seemed to say, "because I've been here all along." She blinked. I blinked in return as I settled back down into the bed, content and happy.

Isn't that so often what happens? It's when we stop frantically searching that we find what we're looking for. It's when we pull back that we discover the prize right in front of us. Sometimes it's best to let go of anxiety when we're reaching out for solutions...for answers...even for God.

*Have you ever had an answer*
*or solution become clear to you*
*after you'd stopped struggling*
*with a problem?*

*Sometimes the best thing to do*
*with a problem is simply step*
*away from it awhile. Go for*
*a walk. . .fix a cup of tea. . .*
*listen to music. . .or, quite*
*literally, "sleep on it."*
*So often the morning light*
*sheds light on our problems,*
*too, and we can see the answer*
*right in front of us.*

**Sometimes the answer comes**
**when we stop searching for it.**

The block of granite,
which was an obstacle in the path of the weak,
becomes a stepping stone in the path of the strong.
-Thomas Carlyle

**Patience is the best remedy for every trouble.**
**-Plautus**

I am convinced that there are times in everybody's
experience when there is so much to be done, that the
only way to do it is to sit down and do nothing.
-Fanny Fern

**Life affords no higher pleasure**
**than that of surmounting difficulties.**
**-Samuel Johnson**

Cast thy burden upon the Lord,
and he shall sustain thee.
-Psalm 55:22

**You must grow in patience when you**
**meet with great wrongs, and they will be**
**powerless to vex your mind.**
**-Leonardo da Vinci**

# THE SHADOW OF THE CAT

J ust as the winter sun was spreading the last afternoon rays across her kitchen floor, Kelli Anderson saw the unmistakable shadow of a cat. The image—husky, round, formidable—slowly lifted itself on all fours and silently slinked into the creeping darkness. Kelli stood transfixed for several minutes after the apparition melted away. She did not have a cat. Her beloved Scoop, an ancient pampered tom, had taken his last breath in her arms six months ago.

Slowly the woman approached the hallway where the shadow had gone. Almost reluctantly she flipped on the light, putting a halt to the fantastical thought that Scoop was back somehow… in some form…and perhaps the darkness held his presence. Her musings shattered as light flooded the hallway…a hallway empty, silent but for the low rumble of the furnace that sat at the bottom of the basement stairs.

Kelli shook her head and managed a bemused smile. "A sign of old age,"she muttered, recalling the ribbings and teasing showered on her when her friends surprised her with a 60th birthday party.

Late the following day, Kelli returned home from work. Again the sun streamed cool, creamy beams of light into her kitchen… and again, out of the corner of her eye, she spotted the shadow. This time it sat on its haunches as cats do, and its head turned in her direction, its face uplifted the way Scoop did when he wanted a treat. No sooner had she looked, the shadow vanished, leaving only the outline of a tote bag she had forgotten to take to work with her.

Late that night, Kelli went upstairs and prepared for bed. Shortly after midnight, she switched off the table lamp and fell into a deep sleep. Suddenly a horrendous screech—the piercing screech of a cat!—yanked her awake, fear drenching her in sweat. It was then she smelled smoke. Panicked, she sprang out of bed, grabbed her bathrobe, slippers, and cell phone. On her way downstairs, she could see heavy black smoke seeping under the door to her kitchen that she had closed earlier. She called 911 as she dashed out the front door. Within minutes, sirens were pulling into her subdivision.

Flames were starting to spread up the stairs when fire fighters extinguished the blaze. "You're lucky," the fire chief told her, "you made it out."

From that day, Kelli never doubted the presence of guardian angels…even when they appear as the shadow of a cat.

*Perhaps you remember a time when a gut feeling moved you away from what turned out to be a bad or dangerous situation. Sometimes, too, an odd coincidence changes the pattern of your day and puts you right where you need to be at exactly the right time. Do you ever attribute these things to God or His guardian angels?*

*Many angels surround you every day, you know. Sometimes they wear the face of the loved one you call the light of your life. . .the physician who brought you back to good health. . .the friend who's always there for you. . .the child who makes you smile. . .the stranger who comes to help you when you need it.*

✺

**At all times, expect the best to happen.**

All God's angels come to us disguised.
-James Russell Lowell


The man who does not believe in miracles surely
makes it certain that he will never take part in one.
-William Blake


He shall give his angels charge over thee,
to keep thee in all thy ways.
-Psalm 91:11


The golden moments in the stream of life
rush past us and we see nothing but sand;
the angels come to visit us,
and we only know them when they are gone.
-George Eliot


Miracles are not contrary to nature,
but only contrary to what we know about nature.
-Augustine

# OLD MARY'S TOM

I can't blame them for thinking I stole Miz Mary's purse. I didn't, but I had a reputation. One night I sneaked out of the house, climbed the fence, and pounded on Miz Mary's bedroom window. She screamed bloody murder. My mom and dad came out to see what happened, and my little brother squealed on me.

Another time I climbed up the tree in front of our house and dropped a water balloon on Miz Mary when she walked by. It landed square on top of her head, and landed me in a heap of trouble. And whenever her old tomcat wandered in our yard, I'd throw rocks at him and send him howling back home. Mind you, I'm not proud of any of this, but I have to tell you so you know why, when Miz Mary's purse disappeared, she accused me, and everyone else did, too.

Turns out she had left it on her porch for a few minutes while she went inside to get something, and when she came back, it was gone. Vanished. And wouldn't you know it, I was alone in the house doing my homework while Mom and Dad were driving my brother to soccer practice, so I didn't have a good alibi.

Miz Mary screamed at me, and I was grilled hard by my mom and dad. When I kept saying I didn't know anything, Miz Mary filled out a police report. That afternoon a patrol car pulled into our driveway, and life as I knew it ended right there. The police couldn't do anything because they didn't have any evidence, but Dad grounded me big time. I had to come right home from school, no sports, no TV, no computer, no nothin'. Even my friend Sammy, who lived in the house behind ours, said his mom told him to keep his distance because now I was "getting into real trouble."

I was miserable. Friday when I came home from school, I dropped my backpack on the back porch, plopped down, and cried. Then Miz Mary's old tomcat showed up, heading right toward me. When I saw him, he stopped in his tracks, ready to bolt. "I'm not gonna throw anything, Old Tom," I muttered. Just like he understood, he came right up to me and sat down, staring at me, like he wanted to tell me something.

The old tom stared and stared. Finally he stood up, started toward the back gate to Sammy's yard, then looked back at me, and I swear he jerked his head at me to follow him. "I'm not supposed to go over there", I said.

Old Tom made that jerk with his head again, so I got up and followed him as far as the gate. Old Tom flattened himself and bellied under the fence and into Sammy's yard. I peered over, watching him as he nosed apart a stand of fountain grass, shot in, and then came out dragging Miz Mary's purse in his teeth! Holy moly! Old Tom dropped it right there on the grass.

"Now what am I going to do?" I thought. If I suddenly know where the purse is, I'm cooked. Who'd believe I didn't throw it there myself? While I was going over my dilemma, Sammy bolted out his back door, then came to a dead stop. He saw me looking over the fence and the purse lying on the ground, and his face turned three shades of red.

"You," I shouted at him. "What…"and my voice trailed off, because I realized that, not only had Sammy taken the purse, but he had let me take the rap. Sammy broke down right there. He came over to the fence and mumbled he was sorry, and that he'd make it right. Then he turned and made a slow head-hanging trudge back to his house. I felt sorry for him—kinda.

There were lots of apologies that day. My parents said how relieved they were, and Miz Mary said she was sorry she flew at me the way she did, and I told her I was sorry for all the pranks I had pulled, and I meant it. But I knew I owed an apology to someone else, too. "Don't worry, kid," I told Old Tom, "if anyone ever bothers you again, you come and tell me, and I'll take care of 'em good!" And I meant that, too.

*Most of us know a relative, neighbor,
teacher, or coworker who always seems
out of sorts. He finds fault and she
never fails to criticize. We know the
problem rests with them and not with
us, yet it's often difficult to cope with
their negativity.*

*When you're in the presence of
negative people, how do you respond?
It's tempting to give them a taste
of their own medicine! But a better
solution begins with forgiveness.
When you respond from a heart of
genuine forgiveness, then words you
choose to say will show the person
a better way. . .a kinder way.*

**The thoughtful things you say and do
Are certain to bounce back to you.**

If you forgive men when they sin against you,
your heavenly Father will also forgive you.
But if you do not forgive men their sins,
your Father will not forgive your sins.
-Matthew 6:14-15 NIV

When you go to bed at night, have for your pillow
three things—love, hope and forgiveness.
And you will awaken in the morning
with a song in your heart.
-Victor Hugo

Life appears to me too short to be spent in nursing
animosity or registering wrongs.
-Charlotte Brontë

Do not seek revenge or bear a grudge against one of
your people, but love your neighbor as yourself.
-Leviticus 19:18 NIV

The best way to knock the chip off your neighbor's
shoulder is to pat him on the back.
-Saying

# THE CATS IN THE WOODS

———•———

The rumor swept through the village. "The Great Pestilence!" the farmer told his family. "And it's cats that bring it. Cats! That's what they say!"

The farmer made sure he had his young daughter's attention. "I don't want you touching cats, you hear?" Clarice nodded, but her mind turned to the gray cat and three kittens she had discovered in the woods the year before.

Their leafy den was her favorite stopping place when she went out gathering berries. Though most people thought cats brought bad luck, Clarice didn't. She liked the soft rumbling sound the gray cat made when she stroked its lean back, and she laughed as the younger cats tumbled over each other in play. Yet she shuddered: plague.

She knew the disease had descended on the land like the wrath of God years before she was born. It began with a purple heaving of the skin, her mother told her, and you surely would be dead before the next Lord's Day. You would be shunned as cursed before God, and only the saints alive on earth would have pity on your cries for help and comfort.

Still, she did not want to tell her parents about the cats' den. That night, Clarice went to bed and mumbled her prayers, fearing God in heaven saw the secret hidden in her heart. She lay awake a long time, listening to her parents' light snoring and also to an unusual sound, as if some little night animal were nibbling at the sturdy wooden walls of the house. At last, Clarice slept.

If she had been outside, Clarice would have seen four pairs of eyes gleaming in the light of the moon, fixed on a shadowy shape busily gnawing a wall of the house. She would have beheld the outlines of a sharply pointed face and thin rodent tail. She would have recognized four cats as they stealthily drew near the rodent, pounced, and disappeared with their prey into the darkness.

In obedience to her father, Clarice never touched the cats again, but stopped to watch when she found them frolicking in the woods. She wondered how such delightful little creatures could bring any harm to anyone. And indeed, it was rats, not cats, that carried the flea responsible for spreading bubonic plague.

Many years later, when Clarice told her granddaughter about the cats in the woods, the young woman wondered if Clarice's compassionate love had kept the family safe through the plague-ridden summer of 1438.

*Today we have more information
at our fingertips than ever before.
Yet an age-old problem persists: what
"everyone knows" proves false, and the
story many claim "really happened"
turns out to be an urban legend.*

*Rumors and tall tales can breed an
atmosphere of needless anxiety, even
distrust and hatred. How do you
guard yourself against the power
of provocative, fear-inducing news,
whether it comes from media or from
friends? It's often difficult to separate
truth from fiction, fact from opinion!*

❧

**A word once spoken flies like the
wind from place to place.**

Test everything. Hold on to the good.
-1 Thessalonians 5:21 NIV

Let thy tender mercies come unto me,
that I may live.
-Psalm 119:77

Whatever is only almost true is quite false,
and among the most dangerous of errors; because
being so near truth, it is the more likely to lead astray.
-Henry Ward Beecher

Serious misfortunes, originating in
misrepresentation, frequently flow and spread before
they can be dissipated by truth.
-George Washington

Every way of a man is right in his own eyes:
but the LORD pondereth the hearts.
-Proverbs 21:2

There is an inmost center in us all
where Truth abides in fullness.
-Robert Browning

# THE INVISIBLE CAT

"One cat I take care of," said Angela, "I've never actually seen." Since I would be gone for several days, Angela had come to talk about my cat-sitting needs. After showing her the locations of food bowls and litter boxes, I started to point out my cat's usual hiding places. That's when she told me about her client with the cat she has been hired to care for repeatedly, yet never seen.

"The food is gone, so I know a cat lives there," Angela continued. "The litter box has been used, and cat toys moved across the floor or from room to room. Every time I go over, I look for him so I can give him some cuddles and play with him for a while, but so far, I haven't been able to find him!"

It's true—not every cat is an adventuresome cat. While some accept guests in the house with equanimity or even excitement, other cats make themselves scarce. Some make friends quickly, begging for strokes and accepting any available lap, while others remain in hiding until the visitors leave and the house is back to normal again.

In many ways, we do the same thing. Some people are thrilled to meet new people and find it easy to strike up a conversation with almost anyone. They're blessed with the ability to put others at ease, creating a warm and caring place for everyone.

But other people identify with the cat that runs and hides the moment Angela enters the door. While they want to meet new people, they find it difficult to initiate a conversation, and they fear what might happen if they were to reach out to someone else. Would that person acknowledge the gesture? Respond in kind? Chances are the answer is "yes."

God created within each of us a heart-deep need for others—for their acceptance, their respect, their admiration, their friendship. The only way we'll ever know the sweetness of another's presence is by coming out of hiding...by stepping out and letting others see who we really are.

*You may know whether you're an extrovert or an introvert. While extroverts are described as outgoing, adventurous, and people-focused, introverts prefer familiar faces and quiet, comfortable surroundings. Of course, few of us are full extroverts or introverts! Even the most outgoing among us needs time alone for reflection and private moments with loved ones. In the same way, extremely introverted individuals grow emotionally stagnant without the introduction of new friends and experiences.*

*Perhaps you notice in yourself something of the extrovert who rarely takes time to care for matters of the soul and spirit. . . or a touch of the introvert who avoids going new places out of anxiety or fear. What can you imagine doing that would expand your horizons?*

**New pleasures come in when we let them in.**

The deepest principle in human nature
is the craving to be appreciated.
-William James

As ye would that men should do to you,
do ye also to them likewise.
-Luke 6:31

A friend is a gift you give yourself.
-Robert Louis Stevenson

Be kind, for everyone you meet
is fighting a hard battle.
-Philo of Alexandria

My only sketch, profile, of Heaven is a large blue sky,
bluer and larger than the biggest I have seen in June,
and in it are my friends—all of them—
every one of them.
-Emily Dickinson

The only way to have a friend is to be one.
-Ralph Waldo Emerson

# CAT COMES HOME

Betsey, the green-eyed white cat, belonged to the Johnsons, as everyone in the neighborhood knew. You would go out to your front porch to find Betsey firmly ensconced in your favorite chair. Dozing in your backyard hammock, you would awaken to discover Betsey contentedly stretched beside you.

The first night she didn't come home for dinner, Jim Johnson was concerned. He searched the yard, and then Jim and his wife set out on foot up and down the block, asking their neighbors if they had seen Betsey lately. Only one had. "I was mowing the lawn a few hours ago," the teenager said. "It looked like she was heading home." But she never arrived.

Weeks passed without a sign of Betsey. Jim and his wife continued their evening walks searching for her, and neighbors kept an eye out for her, but no white cat trotted out from behind a garage or emerged from a stand of tall flowers. Finally the couple had to accept that their beloved Betsey was gone. Later, they adopted a sweet gray kitten who made them smile, but no one could fill the empty spot Betsey had left behind.

An afternoon two years later, after Jim's wife pulled into the driveway, she got out of the car and gathered all the grocery bags she could carry and headed to the door, key in hand. She didn't see the scrawny, scraggly, yellowish creature sitting on the stoop, but heard the screech when she stepped on the tip of its tail. Startled, she backed up and looked down to meet the gaze of two big green eyes. "Betsey!"

Dropping the groceries, she stooped to stroke the bedraggled creature. She opened the door, and Betsey dashed inside. Streaking right past a bewildered gray cat, Betsey hopped up on her favorite chair, circled her cushion, and quickly went to sleep.

No one knew where she had been, but no words could express the joy of her homecoming. Careful brushing and time returned her fur to its natural white, and after weeks of regular meals, she regained her healthy plumpness. From the day she returned, Betsey never again wandered the neighborhood. If you wanted to see her, you needed to look through the large bay window of the Johnsons' home. Betsey would be there, watching the world from her pillow placed on the sill just for her. The sight of the cat would remind you of an important truth: home—physical and spiritual—is a wonderful place to be.

*Have you ever rejoiced at someone's homecoming. . .or returned to your loved ones after a long absence? It's a good feeling to know your loved one has arrived safely. There's nothing like the comfort of your own bed and the familiarity of your home.*

*Spiritually, "home" is the place where we feel most at peace and closest to God. Where is that place for you?*

**Home is where the heart is.**

There is nothing like staying at home
for real comfort.
-Jane Austen

"Return to me," declares the LORD Almighty,
"and I will return to you."
-Zechariah 1:3 NIV

He is the happiest, be he king or peasant,
who finds peace in his home.
-Johann von Goethe

Home is a name, a word, it is a strong one;
stronger than magician ever spoke, or spirit ever
answered to, in the strongest conjuration.
-Charles Dickens

Rejoice with me;
for I have found my sheep which was lost
-Luke 15:6

The greatest thing in the world
is to know how to be one's own self.
-Michel de Montaigne

# A STRONG-WILLED FELINE

"Juno is a strong-willed cat," my sister says, and understates the case. Juniper is the kind of cat who will not take to being on your lap until she jumps into it, in which case she will demand your undivided attention.

She rebuffs your gentle strokes with a resounding hiss unless she has invited your touch, and she'll let you know if she wants to be picked up by winding herself through and around your legs. Today Juno furthered her reputation for intractability. "I let her out to roam the garden while I did some weeding," my sister began. "Though she usually goes in and out through the side door, today we used the front door because I had left my gardening bag on the front porch. Juno followed me and did her usual thing—sniff the grass, bat at a few leaves, and then she settled herself on the patio to soak up the sunshine.

"After about an hour, when I was ready to go in, I put away my gardening things, and then, since Juno didn't budge when I called her, I went over, picked her up, and started toward the front door, because the side door was still locked. She would have nothing of it! That cat howled and fought me with every step I took toward the front door! As soon as I let her down so I could open the door, she took off like a streak around the house and planted herself firmly at the side door. She looked up at it, then at me, then back at the door. I was to get the picture, and fast.

"Since I wasn't interested in another battle, I gave in and did it her way. I entered the front door, walked through the house to the side door, opened it, and watched Juno calmly saunter in looking quite satisfied with herself."

When I recall my sister's story, I wonder how many times I have sat at a door locked to me and howled stubbornly, expecting God to give in to my demands and swing open that door immediately! With cats, such things can happen, as my sister's story shows; but for us mortals, it's better to go where God would take us. He knows where all the open doors are, and will lead us to them, if we only stop fighting and let Him.

*Few of us would want to simply drift along in life, making no effort to reach a goal or work toward an objective. Depending on what we hope to gain, we take the steps we believe will lead us there. But so often, our plans go awry. Unexpected events intervene, and like the GPS device in your car, you're forced to recalculate!*

*It's when we refuse to recalculate— to even change our goal—that we fight God's good plans for us. So often, the detour we must take leads us to a far better opportunity than we could have ever imagined.*

**Make the most of every opportunity that comes your way.**

"For I know the plans I have for you," declares the
LORD, "plans to prosper you and not to harm you,
plans to give you hope and a future."
-Jeremiah 29:11 NIV

**The opportunity that God sends
does not wake up him who is asleep.
-Senegalese proverb**

The world is all gates, all opportunities,
strings of tension waiting to be struck.
-Ralph Waldo Emerson

**The habits of a vigorous mind are formed
in contending with difficulties.
-Abigail Adams**

Opportunity is missed by most people because it is
dressed in overalls, and looks like work.
-Thomas A. Edison

# CAT IN THE CLOSET

———————●———————

Before she leaves her house in the morning, Catherine makes
sure every room and closet door stands ajar. Where wind
through an open window might slam a door shut, Catherine
makes sure there's a doorstop firmly in place. In the wintertime,
when she gathers her hat, coat, and gloves from the hall closet,
she resists the natural tendency to close the door, but instead
leaves it open several inches.

If you have ever lived with a curious cat, you know why
Catherine does these things. Her Siamese, Biscuit, cannot resist
slipping into any newly opened space, even if said space is a
drawer, closet, or cabinet she has investigated many times before.
Whenever Catherine reaches in the pantry for a box of cereal,
Biscuit almost imperceptibly disappears inside, and the door of
the pantry swings shut. Several minutes later, after Catherine has
poured milk on her cereal and opened the newspaper, she hears
plop, plop, plop and plaintive meows coming from the pantry.
Soggy cereal notwithstanding, Catherine gets up to free the cat.
Biscuit emerges, scowling over the fuss and indignity of being
momentarily trapped.

One day Catherine read a story of a kitten in China who wandered unnoticed into a shipping container, only to wind up, skinny and thirsty, in the United States. "That could be Biscuit," she said, laughing. But now, before sealing those boxes of gifts she mails each Christmas to her grandchildren who live 500 miles away, she checks them carefully.

Our impulses, too, can lead us to places that are not easy to get out of. Sometimes our curiosity draws us to follow ill-advised suggestions or enter relationships that leave us hurt and confused. Other times, our impulses overrun our better judgment, and we blurt out an unkind word or spill a secret we later regret. And, too, our own fears, anxieties, and shortcomings can engulf us in the darkness of not knowing where we stand with others or with God.

Like Biscuit, we can find ourselves seemingly "shut" in places where we think there's no escape. But help is as close as a prayer, a call to God to reach out with His hand of forgiveness, love, and compassion. He promises us His presence wherever we are, and what's more, gently and lovingly shows us the way safely out.

*Have you ever found yourself in a
real bind? That is, stuck in a difficult
situation with no good way out.
No matter what you do, someone
will suffer adverse consequences. . .
someone will criticize you. . .
you'll be embarrassed or forced
to face an unappealing outcome.*

*At times like these, true and reliable
guidance comes from above. Can
you think of a time God guided you
through the helpful words of a family
member, friend, or advisor?*

**God works in many ways. . .
but He always works.**

Truly, it is in darkness that one finds the light,
so when we are in sorrow,
then this light is nearest of all to us.
-Meister Eckhart

**I would rather walk with God
in the dark than go alone in the light.
-Mary Gardiner Brainard**

Trust in the LORD with all your heart
and lean not on your own understanding;
in all your ways acknowledge him,
and he will make your paths straight.
-Proverbs 3:5-6 NIV

**Give light and the darkness will disappear of itself.
-Erasmus**

Wherever I am, God is.
-Prayer Card

# A GIFT-BEARING CAT

One spring, things started disappearing. Millie O'Brien forgot to bring in her work gloves from the rose garden, and when she looked for them the next morning, she found only one glove where she was certain she had left two.

"Now what could I have done with it?" she muttered. The baffled gardener searched the area, the potting shed, the garage, and even the house. Finding no glove, she wondered if perhaps this was a sign of age-related memory loss or worse. She told no one else about the incident, because she didn't want to embarrass herself. Little did she know, however, that similar things were happening to her neighbors up and down the block.

Mrs. Daley left her sun visor on a patio chair, only to discover it gone the following day. Amanda Jones hung a hand towel over a railing to dry, and it disappeared, too. Late one night, Jared Miller remembered he'd left his iPad cover on the porch, but figured he'd retrieve it when he left for school the next morning. But by then, it was nowhere to be seen.

Meanwhile, Darrel Henderson, who lived around the corner, couldn't figure out where all the gloves, hats, visors, rags, and sunglasses, and even an iPad cover, were coming from. For several mornings in a row, he awoke to discover some odd item deposited on his front porch. He wondered if there was a neighborhood prankster…or a gaggle of wacky adolescents on the loose…or perhaps a demented kleptomaniac prowling around.

It wasn't until the community summer picnic was held that Darrel had a chance to tell neighbors about the odd assortment of items being deposited on his porch. All at once, voices chimed in, freely confessing the loss of their personal belongings. Now, of course, Darrel feared the neighbors would think he was the demented kleptomaniac!

He quickly went home, gathered all the items in a cardboard box, and returned to the picnic. Millie O'Brien beamed with delight as she snatched her errant garden glove from the box (happy to find the glove, but even happier to dismiss her nagging fears of psychological impairment). Mrs. Daley retrieved her sun visor, Amanda Jones fished out her hand towel, Jared his iPad cover, and several other neighbors their belongings. While everyone reacted with good humor, Darrel Henderson was determined to solve the mystery.

That night, he stayed up later than usual and watched. Finally too sleepy to stay awake, he let his newly adopted cat, Tiger, out. Then he cracked open the window so he'd hear anyone on the porch and proceeded to doze in his chair. Around dawn, he heard something rustling right outside the window. He awoke immediately, flipped on the porch light, and looked. There was Tiger, dragging with him a flip-flop. The cat calmly dropped it by the door, spied Darrel at the window, looked up and meowed as if to say, "Look! I've been out hunting, and here's my prize. Aren't you proud of me?" Then Tiger turned around, and trotted off into the shadows in search of another wonderful gift to bring home.

Mystery solved. The next day, Darrel made sure everyone in the neighborhood knew to come by his house if they were missing anything. Chances are, they'd find it in the basket he'd keep on the porch for all of Tiger's future finds.

When you want to bring a gift to God, He never asks you to scour the countryside for something to bring to Him, and certainly never expects you to offer a gift He hasn't given to you already! All He asks of you is your gratitude and your praise, your prayers, obedience, and love. All He asks of you is—you.

*Do you see that kitten chasing*
*so prettily her own tail?*
*If you could look with her eyes,*
*you might see her surrounded*
*with hundreds of figures performing*
*complex dramas, with tragic*
*and comic issues, long conversations,*
*many characters, many ups*
*and downs of fate.*

-Ralph Waldo Emerson

*Love yearns for love. For what gift could be more important to receive than love from the one to whom we have given our love? What could ever take the place of love? When love is true, it craves, beyond all else, love in return.*

*What experiences in your life have helped you understand the gift of genuine love?*

⁓

**Even more blessed than to receive love is to give love.**

God is love.
-I John 4:8

God loves each of us as if there were only one of us.
-Augustine

When I give, I give myself.
-Walt Whitman

Rings and jewels are not gifts, but apologies for
gifts. The only gift is a portion of thyself.
-Ralph Waldo Emerson

God so loved the world that he gave his one
and only Son, that whoever believes in him
shall not perish but have eternal life.
-John 3:16 NIV

It is in giving oneself that one receives.
-Francis of Assisi

# CATS AND THEIR BFF'S*

E very so often, I hear a story about a cat who has made a completely unexpected friend. For example, I read about Chiquita, a big white cat in Brazil, who befriended a wounded bird. Because of its injuries, the bird would never be able to fly. Chiquita took over the care of the bird, even sharing her food with the little creature. According to Chiquita's human companion, cat and bird are inseparable.

In China, viewers of a TV interview show were entertained by a cat and her best friend, a mouse. The audience watched in amazement as the two frolicked together for the camera, enjoying themselves together without a care in the world.

At a zoo in Russia, Musya, a Siamese cat, nursed two newly born wolf cubs, as their mother produced very little milk. Musya, belonging to a zookeeper's friend, had just delivered a kitten of her own, and she accepted the wolf cubs without question or qualms. Attendants reported that kitten and cubs get along admirably, despite their significant difference in size and temperament. Musya treats all three infants with the same patience and attentiveness.

Some say we look for friends only among those most like ourselves. Sure, we feel more comfortable approaching people we perceive as having similar tastes, values, and interests, as opposed to those who are "different" in some way. But aren't we missing out on some amazing friendships?

It might take a little courage to introduce ourselves to the new neighbor who comes from another country, or the new church member with a background not similar to our own. Some of us may find a person's appearance or age or size or shape so unlike ours that we're willing to let her sit by herself rather than go over and talk to her.

Not every "hello" will develop into a lifelong friendship...but a few might. We can be sure, however, that most all our efforts will ease tension among people and make strangers feel welcome. As we open our world to others, they learn about us and we learn about them. It's the only way we can discover more similarities than differences—more connections than contrasts...more friends than enemies.

Like the cat and her BFF*, we can have some pretty amazing friendships when we're open to them.

*BFF: Best Friend Forever

*It's understandable if you feel most comfortable around people similar to yourself. Yet getting to know someone from outside your circle can yield tremendous benefits, both for you and for the other person. Your similarities open you to understanding and appreciation, and your differences introduce you to new ideas.*

*When was the last time you reached out to someone "different" than yourself and your friends?*

*A true friend can come from anywhere!*

Be not forgetful to entertain strangers: for thereby
some have entertained angels unawares.
-Hebrews 13:2


There is no great difference in the reality of one
country or another, because it is always people you
meet everywhere. They may look different or be
dressed differently, or may have a different
education or position. But they are all the same.
They are all people to be loved.
-Mother Teresa


Do not protect yourself by a fence,
but rather by your friends.
-Czech proverb


Life is not so short but that there is always
time enough for courtesy.
-Ralph Waldo Emerson

# THE CAT WHO'S THERE
# FOR YOU

She called it the worst day of her life. On the last Friday in May, 2009, Marion Henry arrived at the office, and, as usual, she stopped by the cafeteria for a cup of coffee on her way to her cubicle three floors up. Once at her desk, she did what she did every weekday morning: put down the coffee to her right, and lock her purse in a bottom drawer to her left, boot up the computer, sit down, sip coffee, sign in…sip coffee…and read her e-mail.

Marion liked her workday routine, and became quite perturbed if it were interrupted, as it frequently was, by an impromptu meeting or unexpected project. She liked routine in her off-hours, too. Each evening after work, she went directly home, unlocked the door, and delighted in the unfailing presence of Coco, her calico, who greeted her. Marion would pick up Coco for a snuggle, then gently set her down with a hug and a kiss.

Then Coco followed Marion as she went into the kitchen to open a can of cat food for the cat and then fix dinner for herself. They ate in companionable silence. Later, without the annoyance

of an evening meeting to contend with, Marion puttered about
the house with Coco at her heels, then the two curled up on the
sofa and watched TV until it was time to go to bed.

Now on that fateful Friday, just as she reached for another sip
of coffee, Marion noticed an email from a senior manager among
her messages. This was far from routine. In fact, she couldn't
recall ever getting an email from a senior manager in all the years
she had worked for the company. She clicked to open it. This is
what it said:

"Your position has been eliminated due to financial con-
siderations and organizational restructuring. Please report to
Human Resources by 10 a.m. to turn in your badge and sign
release documents. You will receive one week's severance pay for
every year of service. A box has been provided for your personal
belongings, which you will take with you to Human Resources.
We appreciate your association with us, and we wish you all the
best in your future endeavors."

Marion, of course, was stunned. She read the message not
once, but three times. She checked the heading to make sure it
was meant for her. She wondered if this was a coworker's idea of
a joke. She turned, and there by the door of her cubicle, she saw a
corrugated box and a lid she had not noticed before.

Why had her supervisor not talked to her? Then she remembered she was out of town, along with several other supervisors of various departments. Marion stood up, wondering if anyone else had gotten the same or similar message, but saw her coworkers going about their normal morning activities. Was everyone else aware of what was happening to her, and avoiding her? Marion sat back down and read the email once more. Then she calmly shut off her computer, unlocked her drawer and took out her purse. She opened it and reached for the two photographs on her desk—one of Coco as a kitten and another taken recently of the cat curled on her favorite chair. Marion took one last look around her cubicle, then left for Human Resources without saying a word to anyone.

Coco must have heard the key in the door, because when Marion entered so many hours before her usual time, Coco was there to greet her. But the cat did not jump into her arms to snuggle, but stopped short when she saw Marion's face. Coco waited, looking quizzically at Marion, as if trying to figure out what had happened. The cat unobtrusively followed Marion—no winding around her legs as she usually did—as Marion went to the living room and dropped into a chair. There she put her head in her hands and began to cry.

While she wept, Coco sat at her feet. When Marion had no tears left, the woman finally looked up. That's when Coco jumped lightly into her lap, gently nudging her, licking away the tear drops still rolling down her face. Marion wrapped her arms around the cat, and they sat that way for a long, long time.

Life for Marion and Coco was far from routine for several months while Marion sorted through her options and at last found another position. A new routine emerged, and the days and years passed happily for both human and cat.

As she reflected back on the worst day of her life, Marion was amazed to discover that for Coco, it was a day of concern and caring. It was a day the cat did not beg for food, or jump into her arms for attention, or go into her toy basket and drag out a catnip mouse to show her. No, it was a day to comfort Marion. It was a day to help someone heal. It was a day to lick away tears. Yes, the cat you love and who loves you knows your moods and feels your sorrows. The understanding silence and compassionate presence of a cat can make all the difference.

*Cats respond to human moods
and emotions, as most cat lovers
will tell you. When you're not
feeling well, your cat might spend
the day snuggled up to you while
you rest, ignoring his regular spot
by the window. When you're
happy, your cat picks up on that,
too, and will want to get in on
the excitement.*

*Perhaps you can think of a time
when someone seemed to know
exactly how you felt. Compassion
without a hint of judgment is just
one of the many ways we can
show kindness.*

❧

**There's no better physician then
someone who cares.**

I would rather feel compassion
than know the meaning of it.
-Thomas Aquinas

I expect to pass through life but once.
If therefore, there be any kindness I can show,
or any good thing I can do to any fellow being,
let me do it now, and not defer or neglect it,
as I shall not pass this way again.
-William Penn

If we cannot be clever, we can always be kind.
-Alfred Fripp

Those who bring sunshine to the lives
of others cannot keep it from themselves.
-James M. Barrie

True benevolence, or compassion, extends itself
through the whole of existence and sympathizes with
the distress of every creature capable of sensation.
-Joseph Addison

# CATS WITH CREDENTIALS

W hile you may have worked hard to earn your educational credentials, there is a cat who has received a degree without ever cracking (or clawing) a book. The story goes that a law enforcement officer, looking into a college suspected of offering fake degrees, enrolled his cat, Colby Nolan. On the application, the officer listed community college courses Colby had supposedly taken, along with a modest amount of work experience. Colby was accepted as a student, and for a mere $299, the cat received a bachelor's degree in business administration.

The degree-granting institution wasn't finished with Colby yet, however, inviting him to apply for an executive MBA for an additional $100. How could any smart, well-educated cat refuse such an offer? Colby didn't. He was awarded an MBA, along with a transcript showing he had earned a 3.5 grade point average.

While Colby gained, the diploma mill lost, being fined and shut down the following year.

Other felines also have a piece of sheepskin to hang on their scratching post. There's Oreo Collins, a tuxedo cat, who was granted a diploma from an online high school as part of a sting operation, and George, a cat in Britain who is registered with several professional organizations and is an accredited hypnotherapist. In the same field of study is feline Zoe D. Katze, now Dr. Katze, whose achievements led to a full investigation into credentialing scams.

Fortunately, the cats took little notice of their exalted status in academic and professional circles, and instead went on about their day being cats. Perhaps, during a long nap in the garden, one of them may have wondered about all the fuss suddenly surrounding him, but yawned and went back to sleep. Another may have seen all the cameras pointed in her direction, and nonchalantly walked off.

After all, any cat knows the difference between a live mouse and a toy mouse, and the right way and the wrong way to go about catching, or playing with, said mouse. A cat knows these things, because he's perfectly content to be exactly who he is at all times.

*In the past, you would need to travel far from your hometown to assume a new identity or make false claims about yourself. Now, however, you need travel no further than your nearest computer! Online, you can describe yourself in whatever terms you choose, and only those who know you will see through the sham.*

*Does what you say about yourself match the person you really are?*

❦

**Truth and honesty make for soft pillows and sweet dreams.**

Honesty is the first chapter in the book of wisdom.
-Thomas Jefferson

**I cannot comprehend how any man**
**can want anything but the truth.**
**-Marcus Aurelius**

It is the chiefest point of happiness
that a man is willing to be what he is.
-Erasmus

**If God had wanted me otherwise,**
**He would have created me otherwise.**
**-Johann von Goethe**

The voice of conscience is so delicate
that it is easy to stifle it; but it is also clear
that it is impossible to make it.
-Madame de Staël

# THE MIRACULOUS
# BEGINNINGS OF CATS

Though domestic cats aren't mentioned in the Bible, they played an important role on Noah's ark, according to legend. It seems that Noah, after watching a pair of mice and a pair of rats enter the vessel, became concerned that the creatures would gnaw through the wood of the ark and cause a leak. That's definitely something he wanted to avoid, and rightly so.

Just as Noah was wondering what to do, a pair of lions proceeded up the gangplank. "King of beasts," Noah called, "perhaps you can help me with my problem." The lions stopped and listened as Noah explained. When he finished speaking, the lions looked at each other, then they both breathed in deeply and released a huge aaaachooooo! (almost blowing away a pair of tiny grasshoppers walking by at that moment).

Out of each lion's nostrils popped a frisky kitten, one a male and the other a female. The kittens stretched and meowed and friskily followed the lions into the safety of the ark. For the 40 days and 40 nights it rained, and for the many months the ark floated in the water, the kittens made sure the mice and rats resisted their natural urge to gnaw on wood and so thwart God's plan to save Noah, his family, and the animals.

The Biblical account of Noah and the ark illustrates God's desire to save, and the fanciful legend of the lions and kittens reveals a very human need to amuse and entertain. Can't you imagine this bit of folklore stemming from a son's question to his father as they sat for long hours fishing on the lake? Or from a daughter's query to her mother as they spent the afternoon preparing the family's meal?

Stories then and now weave through every culture, allowing creative imaginations to roam and discover…to think deeply and reach high into the unknown and beyond. Many say stories tell us much about ourselves. What we might draw from the tale of the pair of lions who sneezed a pair of kittens might be this: people of ancient times—just like us—enjoyed a story that made them smile.

> *For I will consider my Cat Jeoffry…*
> *For in his morning orisons*
> *he loves the sun and the sun loves him.*
> *For he is of the tribe of Tiger…*
> *For there is nothing sweeter*
> *than his peace when at rest.*
> *For there is nothing brisker*
> *than his life when in motion.*

-Christopher Smart

*How long has it been since*
*you've read a story to a child. . .*
*or woven a narrative from the*
*shape of a cloud or the pattern*
*of stars in the nighttime sky?*
*Few of us say we have time for*
*such dawdling. . .but very few*
*of us would say such things*
*aren't worthwhile.*

*Stories connect lives. . .*
*express dreams. . .*
*warm hearts. . .bring smiles.*
*What's a story you'd like to tell?*

**Take time to unleash your
creative spirit.**

He that is of a merry heart hath a continual feast.
-Proverbs 15:15

**Moonlight is sculpture.**
**-Nathaniel Hawthorne**

The real act of discovery consists not in finding new
lands but in seeing with new eyes.
-Marcel Proust

**The Possible's slow fuse is lit by the Imagination.**
**-Emily Dickinson**

Mirth is God's medicine.
Everybody ought to bathe in it.
-Henry Ward Beecher

**The invariable mark of wisdom**
**is to see the miraculous in the common.**
**-Ralph Waldo Emerson**

There are no rules of architecture
for a castle in the clouds.
-G. K. Chesterson

# THE WATCH CAT

Shirley, devoted to her matronly calico cat Missy, told me she was thinking about adopting a dog. I could understand why. She lives alone, and there had been some thefts and even a home invasion reported around the neighborhood that summer. I agreed that a dog might prove a good deterrent to the casual burglar, and further, would alert her to anyone trying to break in during the night.

Then we discussed how Missy would react to a dog in the house, and we agreed: "Not well." Missy, thoroughly spoiled by her doting human, snarled through the window at any cat wandering across the yard. Once, when a friend brought her poodle into Shirley's living room, Missy tore upstairs and wouldn't come down for days. Fearing a major problem with the cat, Shirley put off getting a dog.

Now Missy was a sociable cat, but clearly a "one-person" cat, and that one person was Shirley. Just as Missy howled at any animal spied on her domain, she would growl loudly at two-legged interlopers. Somehow the cat recognized the sound of Shirley's sister's car pulling in the driveway, and would not growl at all, but instead trot to the door to greet her. Same with Shirley's friends who came to visit.

The approach of a person delivering a parcel or someone scouting the neighborhood for tree-trimming or remodeling work, however, elicited an immediate reaction from Missy, who would rush to the hallway and scream at the front door. Shirley knew to get up and go to the door, as the bell was about to ring. The cat was never wrong.

One night late in the summer when the nights were still warm, Shirley went to bed, forgetting to close the sliding glass door leading to her backyard deck. In the early hours of the morning, she was awakened to Missy's sharp cry and an extraordinary dog-like growl coming from the rear of the house. Shirley heard Missy unmistakable gallop as she plowed through the living room and hallway to reach her bedroom, where the cat jumped on Shirley's bed, growling, agitated beyond anything Shirley had ever seen. Terrified, Shirley flipped on a light, leaped out of bed, grabbed her robe and cellphone and ran to the living room, Missy at her heels.

All was quiet and seemingly undisturbed. Still clutching her phone, Shirley turned on a lamp. It was then she noticed a slight ripple of the curtain drawn across the sliding door. Her heart pounding, she approached the door, now remembering she had forgotten to close and latch it before going to bed. She peeked out to see a shadowy figure retreating through the shrubbery. She put her hand in the opening where the prowler had started to cut the screen.

Shirley knew she had no need for a dog as long as she had Missy. And Missy, who could have told her she never needed a dog, remains to this day the sole claimant to Shirley's love and attention.

Who can doubt the time-honored truth that what we want is often something we already have? Appearances may fool us for a time, but when we really think about it, we realize that what we've been looking for has been right there all along.

It is impossible for a lover of cats to
banish these alert, gentle, and discriminating friends,
who give us just enough of their regard and
complaisance to make us hunger for more.
-Agnes Repplier

**Love is enough. Why should we ask for more?**
**-Ella Wheeler Wilcox**

Nature arms each man with some faculty
which enables him to do easily some
feat impossible to any other.
-Ralph Waldo Emerson

Most often, we already have everything we require. There's no need to buy more, get more, or search for more...including for spiritual things.

Someone once said, "The search for God is always futile, because God can never be found—simply because God has never been lost." How true! We need never pursue His presence, because His presence is with us, no matter where we are.

❧

*I bear no worry, stress, or care*
*Because I know my God is there.*

The great blessings of mankind are within us,
and within our reach; but we shut our eyes and,
like people in the dark, fall foul upon the very thing
we search for, without finding it.
-Seneca

While a man is contented with himself
and his own resources, all is well.
-William Hazlitt

Simplicity, simplicity, simplicity!
I say, let your affairs be as two or three,
and not a hundred or a thousand….We are happy in
proportion to the things we can do without.
-Henry David Thoreau

How many things are there which I do not want.
-Socrates

# MAGICAL CATS

The Cat Theatre of Moscow stars some truly exceptional cats. The troupe of 120 cats—many of them rescued from the street—perform tricks of all kinds in specially written skits, along with human mimes and assistants.

But can you actually train a cat? No, says their handler—cats will do only what they want to do, as anyone who has been around cats could tell you. Instead, their human counterparts work with them to determine the movements individual cats will take to naturally and consistently. The actors then build the show around what the cats are likely to do, given a few gentle prompts. Among the cats are many willing and able to perform marvelous tricks, like handstands and acrobatics, or walking across the stage perched on a giant ball or across a bar or tightrope.

Of course, just because a cat can do something doesn't mean he will do it. Sometimes the feline stars improvise on the spot, leaving their two-legged colleagues to figure out the next move for themselves. Watching the video on YouTube, I marveled at the cats' abilities. But in my house, I think the cats are the ones doing the prompting, and I the tricks. Before I reach the kitchen,

Smokey has jumped up on the counter and stands waiting for her breakfast of canned paté. If I dare first fix the coffee, she meows loudly to let me know I'm not doing what I'm supposed to do. If the supply of kibble is low, Buttercup will plant herself next to the bowl and stare at me until I get the hint and fill it.

Later in the day, when I sit to read, Callie jumps in my lap, prompting me with nudges and purrs that it's time to brush her. In the evening, Indy jumps up and waits in the middle of the bed, watching me until I finally crawl in—then she curls up and goes to sleep. Yes, clearly these cats are running the show.

Although I can't imagine any one of them being inclined to walk a tightrope, they delight me with their presence, and they bless my life in so many ways. I can think of no better stress-reliever than a purring cat in my lap, and no quieter, calmer companion than a cat snoozing on the rug at my feet as I work for hours at my desk. I don't mind at all doing the things they've trained me to do!

We rarely know what we're
capable of doing until we're asked
to do it. Sometimes we take it
upon ourselves to test our limits;
at other times adversity or
hardship enters our lives, and
we're required to reach beyond
our boundaries.

Have you ever been surprised at
your capabilities when up against
a challenge? Chances are, you
"performed" better than you ever
thought you could!

❧

**Do, and be surprised how
much you can do.**

It is our duty as men and women to proceed
as though the limits of our abilities do not exist.
-Pierre Teilhard de Chardin


God gives us always strength enough,
and sense enough, for everything He wants us to do.
-John Ruskin


Let us remember that within us
there is a palace of immense magnificence.
-Teresa of Avila


I can do all things through Christ which strengtheneth me.
-Philippians 4:13


Never grow a wishbone, daughter,
where your backbone ought to be.
-Clementine Paddleford


To measure up to all that is demanded of him,
a man must overestimate his capacities.
-Johann von Goethe

# WHAT A CAT HEARS

Ann Marie's household included seven cats, each one having wandered onto her rural lot. Once there, they had found themselves a forever home. The generous woman came to believe that wandering cats, like hoboes of decades past, left messages on fence posts for one another, such as, "Do not enter—loose dog," or "Go to porch. Look cute. Door opens. Food for life."

Of course, Ann Marie didn't really believe cats could read (or write), but one eerie event drew her to this conclusion: they certainly understood English.

Before Ann Marie allowed a new cat or kitten inside the house, she took the creature to her cousin, a veterinarian, who checked and vaccinated the animal. From then on, the cat could live indoors, and she took each cat to the doctor yearly.

Now Ann Marie knew not to bring out the carrier too soon, because all cats would vanish in an instant. Instead, on appointment day, she quickly grabbed the unsuspecting patient and secured the howling cat in the carrier for the ride to the clinic.

One day Ann Marie phoned the clinic about bringing in Patches, who appeared ill. "She doesn't seem to be interested in food lately," Ann Marie said, "and she's been following me around, which is unusual. In fact she's here at my feet right now. I'm concerned there's something wrong."

The receptionist managed to squeeze in an appointment the following hour, and Ann Marie took it. Then she looked down to where Patches was—and she wasn't. Patches had disappeared. Ann Marie started searching, and she located every cat but the one she needed. Generally, the cats paced nervously whenever Ann Marie became stressed, but this time the snoozing cats barely opened an eyelid in response to Ann Marie's increasingly frantic search.

After 45 minutes of looking, Ann Marie called the clinic, beside herself with apologies. "I don't know how she knew!" Then Ann Marie remembered: Patches had been in the same room—listening!—as she set up the appointment.

"She's a lot like me," Ann Marie told her cousin later in the week when she came into the clinic with Patches firmly in her arms. "There are times I just want to hide…but somehow responsibility always finds me!" They laughed. And Ann Marie decided she'd send the clinic a text message the next time she needed an appointment.

*Some things just aren't fun—*
*and doctor's appointments might*
*be only one example. There are*
*tedious but essential tasks around*
*the house. . .uncomfortable but*
*necessary discussions with a loved*
*one. . .wearisome but obligatory*
*responsibilities to take care of.*
*We're often tempted to put them*
*off as long as possible!*

*Are you procrastinating on*
*something you know needs doing?*

**The first step is the hardest.**

Delay always breeds danger,
and to protract a great design is often to ruin it.
-Miguel de Cervantes

**For purposes of action,**
**nothing is more useful than narrowness of thought**
**combined with energy of will.**
**-Henri Frederic Amiel**

If deeds are wanting,
all words appear mere vanity and emptiness.
-Greek proverb

**Encourage one another daily,**
**as long as it is called Today.**
**-Hebrews 3:13 NIV**

Can anything be sadder than work unfinished?
Yes: work never begun.
-Christina Rossetti

**The wise man does at once**
**what the fool does finally.**
**-Baltasar Gracian**

# CATS OF HOPE

In the weeks following the events of September 11, 2001, a news item emerged of cats who had survived the destruction of the World Trade Center. Apparently a mother cat and her kittens were discovered in the rubble of one of the towers, nestled in a carton of napkins. Though it's hard to say whether the little family was living someplace in the tower when it collapsed, or if mama had found shelter there in the days following the collapse, the story brings to mind our longing to find a ray of hope in the gloom of sadness.

The ability—the willingness—to find light in the night, even if it's a single candle shining in profound darkness, enables us to embrace peace, hope, and healing. Those tiny lives amid the rubble convince us that the mystery of life survives, despite the ravages of death, and that rebirth and renewal is an integral part of nature.

In our personal losses and disappointments, we cherish the tiny eyes of new life we find when we look beneath the rubble… the soft, sweet breath of rejuvenation we feel as we rest in the embrace of God's continuing love.

The cats' rescuers named the mama cat Hope, and her kittens they named Amber, Flag, and Freedom. Today, though over a decade away from the date of our national loss—and heart-wrenching personal loss for many—we will never forget the sorrow. But at the same time, we will keep our eyes and heart open to the gift of life....because it's there...always.

*Hope is the thing with feathers*
*That perches in the soul.*
*And sings the tune*
*Without the words,*
*And never stops at all.*

-Emily Dickinson

*Most of us can remember
what we were doing on
September 11, 2001,
when we first heard what
had happened in New York
City. . .at the Pentagon in
Virginia. . .over a field in
Pennsylvania. What other
events in your life do you
remember vividly? What
gives you hope to move
through dark times?*

෴

**Memories are the stories
gathered for a lifetime.**

Emergencies have always been necessary to progress.
It was darkness which produced the lamp. It was fog
that produced the compass. It was hunger that drove
us to exploration. And it took a depression
to teach us the real value of a job.
-Victor Hugo

I am come that they might have life,
and that they might have it more abundantly.
-John 10:10

If we had no winter, the spring would not be so
pleasant; if we did not sometimes taste of adversity,
prosperity would not be so welcome.
-Anne Bradstreet

In the deepest night of trouble and sorrow God
gives us so much to be thankful for that we need
never cease on singing.
-Samuel Taylor Coleridge

He that wrestles with us strengthens our nerves and
sharpens our skill. Our antagonist is our helper.
-Edmund Burke

# THE CATS' BREAKFAST

Two of my cats prefer dry food. If I keep their bowls full, they are happy. Whatever I buy seems to satisfy them, as the bowls empty once a day regardless of what brand or flavor of crunchy morsels I buy.

The other two cats, however, prefer canned food, and they are finicky eaters. If I put in a supply of the brand and flavor that has been their favorite for the last three days, now, of course, it's a disgusting recipe. I spoon it out, and they look at me with accusation in their eyes, and then treat me to a full view of their backside as they saunter out of the kitchen.

For these two cats, gratitude is not on the radar. To this day, they have no compunction letting me know how they feel about their "daily bread." If I buy a mix of flavors and brands, it's clear when I haven't opened the right one. Sometimes, what's approached with alacrity in the morning is snubbed in the evening, despite the fact the food has come from the same can. I'm certain that what I throw away in uneaten food would feed several other cats for a lifetime.

"Do you realize," I say as I rinse the last mouthful down the sink, "that there are cats who are hungry—famished, even—and who would give their last shred of fur to have this food?" My cats obviously don't care. They sit in the middle of the kitchen floor glaring at me until I open another can of food—which may or may not prove the right one.

Gratitude for food is something I try to remember every day. In honor of the people who are hungry, I give thanks for the meal on our table. If I start complaining because my grocer hasn't stocked the item I want, I think of my friend in a faraway country who rejoices if she comes home with basic supplies. If I grumble because of rising prices, I stop when I think of the woman for whom rising prices means not going without a pastry, but without milk and eggs.

"Give us this day our daily bread" we petition in The Lord's Prayer...and how blessed we are, because few of us have ever needed to ask twice.

*When we're open to
learning, our lessons can
come from anyone or
anywhere—including
the antics of a finicky cat.
Sometimes, they're the ones
that stick with us the most
and teach us what God
would have us to know.*

*What simple truths have
you gleaned from common,
everyday occurrences?*

**A thankful heart finds
blessings every day.**

O give thanks unto the Lord; for he is good:
because his mercy endureth for ever.
-Psalm 118:1

If the only prayer you ever say in your entire life is
"Thank you," that would suffice.
-Meister Eckhart

Ingratitude is a kind of weakness;
the clever are never ungrateful.
-French proverb

Would you know who is the greatest saint in the
world? It is not he who prays most or fasts most;
it is not he who gives most alms...but it is he
who is always thankful to God.
-William Law

Eden is that old fashioned house we dwell in every day
without suspecting our abode until we drive away.
-Emily Dickinson

Be glad of life because it gives you the chance to love,
and to work, and to play and to look up at the stars.
-Henry Van Dyke

# THE CONTEMPLATIVE CAT

If you have ever seen a cat sit peacefully, focusing on nothing in particular yet seeing everything, you can imagine why ancient Asian people honored the cat as a symbol of deep contemplation. Cats roamed their temples both as mousers and as inspirational presences to remind harried visitors to slow their pace.

Today, it's hard not to envy the sleek housecat her relaxed and seemingly reflective life. She knows how to settle in a shaft of sunlight, stretch, and let the warmth embrace her. She finds a comfortable corner and places herself there—not to read, watch TV, or chat with friends—but to look at the room as if studying every lamp, chair, rug, and pillow.

In the morning, the cat goes to an open window to sniff the cool, fresh air as her way of greeting the day. No catching up on the news, rushing to get ready for work, or hastily grabbing something to eat and running out the door! No, she will find her way to nourishment when she's ready.

In the evening, she locates her resting spot, circles several times, and then lowers herself gently into position. A thorough bathing routine takes place—never hurried, never cut short with a phone call or the memory of one last thing to do—but everything in order, in its time. She assesses her work, and satisfied, puts her head down and goes to sleep.

While our human responsibilities call us away from such a strictly contemplative existence, surely the cat's example reminds us that time away from our to-do list might allow us to experience a little bit of her peace. A silenced phone and a shut-off laptop could go a long way to giving us the distance our hearts and minds require for a balanced perspective and clear thinking. In many ways, we would do well to copy the contemplative cat.

*One clover, and a bee.*
*And revery.*
*The revery alone will do,*
*if bees are few.*
*-Emily Dickinson*

*It's easy to get into the situation of doing too much. . .expecting more accomplishment from yourself than humanly possible, and then feeling down on yourself because you have "failed." Have you ever found this to be true?*

*A daily time set aside for prayer, meditative reading, and quiet contemplation gives you the mental and emotional space you need to make realistic choices about what you are able to do, given the time and other resources available to you.*

**Sometimes a little rest is best.**

Contemplation places us in a purity and radiance which
is far above our understanding.
-John Ruysbroeck

**Meditation is the life of the soul.**
**-Francis Quarles**

Remember the sabbath day, to keep it holy.
-Exodus 20:8

**Meditation is the tongue of the soul**
**and the language of our spirit.**
**-Jeremy Taylor**

We live longer than our forefathers; but we suffer more
from a thousand artificial anxieties and cares.
They fatigued only the muscles,
we exhaust the finer strength of the nerves.
-Edward George Bulwer-Lytton

**Meditation is a rich and powerful method of study**
**for anyone who knows how to examine his mind.**
**-Michel de Montaigne**

# RESILIENT CATS

As if by a miracle, cats and kittens have survived harrowing situations. Take a kitten named Flowerpot by her rescuers. The tiny tortoiseshell had slipped into a shipping container in Malaysia and spent the next several weeks in transit to England. It's believed she survived by lapping condensation that had formed on the walls of the sealed crate. Though thin and dazed, she greeted startled workers in Salisbury with a friendly meow, and has since made her home in her new country.

Another cat's face peered out from a most unexpected place—a block of ice. A motorist in Minnesota noticed a big chunk of ice on the road, and then spotted a cat's face inside. The motorist stopped to examine the ice, expecting the cat to have been frozen to death until she heard the animal meow. That's when she picked up the ice chunk and took it to a vet, who carefully thawed the ice and released the cat trapped inside. The cold cat regained not only his life, but earned a warm home with the motorist.

In England, a tabby wandered into an electricity sub-station and received an 11,000-volt shock when he decided to check out a live terminal. A worker managed to pull him away from the terminal and get immediate treatment for his burned paws, singed fur, and paralyzed ears and front leg. Named Sparky by the worker, the cat's escape from death was extraordinary, in that a shock like the one he took was capable of killing a human being.

Amazing survival stories abound about cats—and people. We often go through experiences we would have said we could never survive—but we do. Often, these are the experiences that show us our own strength of body and spirit, because our capabilities have been tested to the limit, and have proven sound. These, too, are the things that enable us to feel empathy and compassion for others going through the same or similar experience, and that makes us into people who can help others with genuine understanding, practical assistance, and real-life encouragement.

Few of us would ever invite accident or illness, hardship or tragedy into our lives, but as with the cat trapped in a shipping crate, sometimes these things happen when we're simply going about our daily activities. Sometimes we're just taking a look at something, and we get more than we bargained for.

We end up at a place in life we thought we'd never set foot—but there we are. We heard about such things happening, and we never thought they'd happen to us—but they did.

God permits us to be there, or intends for us to be right where we are. For what purpose? That's another amazing story—one we discover sometimes sooner…sometimes later…but there's always a God-blessed purpose. Of that, we can be sure.

*I am the true vine, and my Father is the gardener. He cuts off every branch in me that bears no fruit, while every branch that does bear fruit he prunes so that it will be even more fruitful.*
*-John 15:1-2 NIV*

*You cannot create experience. You must undergo it.*
*-Albert Camus*

*Adversity is not without many comforts and hopes.*
*-Francis Bacon*

Difficulties are God's errands; and when we are sent upon them, we should esteem it a proof of God's confidence— as a compliment from Him.
-Henry Ward Beecher

If all our misfortunes were laid in one common heap, whence everyone must take an equal portion, most people would be content to take their own and depart.
-Socrates

Prosperity is too apt to prevent us from examining our conduct; but adversity leads us to think properly of our state, and so is most beneficial to us.
-Samuel Johnson

Many a man curses the rain that falls upon his head, and knows not that it brings abundance to drive away hunger.
-Basil the Great

The harder the conflict, the more glorious the triumph. What we obtain too cheap, we esteem too lightly; 'tis dearness only that gives everything its value.
-Thomas Paine

*We like to hear about heroes
because their stories inspire us
to believe in the human capacity
for courage. . .compassion. . .
unconditional love. . .even the
ultimate sacrifice. Heroes make
a difference for the good, and we
admire them for it.*

*You may not think of yourself
as a hero, but you are a hero. . .
perhaps to the loved one you
have always cared for. . .
the coworker you helped out. . .
the friend you encouraged. . .
the stranger you befriended.
If you have done any of these
things, you have made a difference for the good in someone's
life. . .and in your own.*

**Those who take the time to care
are heroes in the eyes of others.**

Self-sacrifice is the real miracle
out of which all the reported miracles grow.
-Ralph Waldo Emerson

Events that are predestined require but little
management. They manage themselves. They slip into
place while we sleep, and suddenly we are aware that
the thing we fear to attempt, is already accomplished.
-Amelia Barr

Men often bear little grievances with less courage than
they do large misfortunes.
-Aesop

Affliction comes to us all, not to make us sad, but
sober; not to make us sorry, but to make us wise; not to
make us despondent, but by its darkness to refresh us.
-Henry Ward Beecher

# THE CATS WITH SIX TOES

———●———

The mid-twentieth century novelist Ernest Hemingway was particularly fond of polydactyl cats. These cats, commonly known as mitten cats or snowshoe cats, possess one or more extra toes on at least one of their paws.

Non-polydactyl cats have 18 toes, five on each front paw and four on each back paw; polydactyl cats might have six toes on a single paw, or even as many as seven toes on one or more paws. Polydactylism is genetically inherited—at least one parent must have the condition before a kitten can be born with it.

Long before Ernest Hemingway took a special fondness to the cats, polydactyls were especially prized on ships because of their extraordinary hunting abilities. Their extra claw or claws gave them superior traction on wet, slippery decks, and sailors believed they brought good luck and ensured safe travel across rough and treacherous seas. It's commonly believed that Hemingway was given his first polydactyl cat, a white tom, by a ship's captain he met on one of his voyages across the Atlantic.

Hemingway took the polydactyl cat, whom he named Snowball, to his home in Key West, Florida, where the tom did what toms do. Soon the island boasted a sizable population of polydactyl kittens. The author enjoyed naming the kittens after various film and literary figures, as polydactyls generally respond to their names and are known to be quite smart (often able to open doors and latches, due to their extra toe) and very people-friendly.

A passionate cat-lover, the author made certain the cats would be looked after in the years ahead, and his will stipulated that the cats on his estate would receive continuing care. The author died in 1961, and since then, his home in Key West has been inhabited by a succession of writers and artists, as well as over 50 descendants of Snowball, most of whom are polydactyl. The estate is now the Ernest Hemingway Home and Museum, and it's open to the public. In accordance with the author's wishes, all cats are well cared for and roam freely about the small island.

While Hemingway and generations of cat aficionados adore the polydactyl cat, the cat is not considered a show-worthy animal because of its abnormal number of toes. How like those who look the other way when a person with a visible disability enters the room. No, they don't look like everyone else… which just might make them very special in the eyes of God.

*It's only natural to note a
person's appearance—after
all, it's the first thing we see,
and it's the way we identify
the person in our mind.
Willingness, however,
to look beyond an obvious
distinguishing characteristic
and meet the person inside
can bring delightful surprises
and extraordinary blessings.
For some, it's brought a
friend. . .a teacher. . .an
inspiration. . .even a spouse.*

*What are your reactions
when you meet a person
with obvious disabilities?
How do you think he or she
feels in your presence?*

**A heart of kindness never
fears to love.**

To live without loving is not really to live.
-Molière

Love should be as natural as living and breathing.
-Mother Teresa

This is my commandment,
That ye love one another, as I have loved you.
-John 15:12

There are no little events in life;
those we think of no consequence may be full of fate,
and it is at our own risk if we neglect the acquaintances
and opportunities that seem to be casually offered,
and of small importance.
-Amelia Barr

A man doesn't learn to understand
anything unless he loves it.
-Johann Von Goethe

# CAT TRACKS

For years, Margery owned and managed a successful gift shop in a small town outside Albuquerque, New Mexico. Part of the appeal of the shop was Swoop, a tawny cat that had been at the shop since her kittenhood. Every morning, Swoop could be seen sitting in the window watching passersby from the comfort of a big, comfy pillow placed there especially for her. Later, as business picked up, she would wander the aisles, rubbing against the legs of congenial shoppers. Sometimes Swoop would hop up onto a display shelf of plush animals and lie among them as still as the tiger and panda bear next to her. She seemed inordinately pleased with herself when she stretched out a paw and elicited a shriek from a startled shopper.

Then came the day that Margery received a call from a hospital in Phoenix, Arizona, where her mother lived. Her mother, a widow, had fallen and broken her hip, and as the only child, Margery quickly put her assistant in charge of the shop and flew to Phoenix.

It didn't take long for Margery to realize that her mother would no longer be able to live alone in her house. Sure, her mother could move to an assisted living apartment, but the look of sadness and resignation on the aged lady's face broke her daughter's heart. Getting a reliable person to come to her mother's home each day to help with baths, meals, and housework seemed nothing less than an ongoing headache. So Margery did what her sense of love and duty compelled her to do: she flew back to Albuquerque, sold the shop to her assistant, and in less than a month, she was on her way back to her childhood home in Arizona, taking Swoop with her.

After the 400-mile drive and a day confined in a kennel, Swoop was not a happy cat. When Margery took her inside the house and released her, Swoop sniffed suspiciously and seemed reluctant—or too frightened—to explore. Margery thought it might be a good idea to take the cat to one room, along with her food, water, and litter box, and shut the door until she could become acclimated to her new surroundings. After she settled the cat, she went about the business of unpacking and settling in. The next morning she would go to the nursing home where her mother was staying and bring her home.

Everything went as planned, and both mother and daughter began this next stage of their lives together. After two or three days of cajoling from both women, Swoop ventured out of the room and cautiously began exploring the house. Then one day a few weeks later, Swoop was nowhere to be found.

Marjory searched everywhere, looking for a cupboard or cranny that would harbor a cat with a mind to hide, but she found no sign of Swoop. She told her neighbors up and down the street to please watch for a tawny cat wandering scared in an unfamiliar place. She put up a photo and "Lost Cat" notice on a corner light post, at the local veterinary clinic, and on the supermarket bulletin board. She looked and looked for weeks, but without success.

Two months later, Margery received a call from her former assistant, now owner of the gift shop. "Margery!" she cried into the phone, breathless with excitement. "It's Swoop! She was right by the front door waiting for me when I unlocked the shop this morning! I can't believe my eyes, but it's Swoop! She walked right in, meowed, and walked straight to the back of the store where she used to have her food and water bowls!"

Margery was dumbfounded. "Swoop found her way back to Albuquerque—400 miles? How'd she do it?"

"I don't know," the assistant replied, "but she did. There's no mistaking—she's here, looking up at me right now, wondering why her bowls aren't where they're supposed to be!"

This is a remarkable story, but not an unusual one. Cats have been known to travel hundreds of miles to return to a house they once lived in. No one quite knows how they navigate their way over long distances—perhaps it's scent, perhaps it's instinct, perhaps it's built-in GPS. Some feline travelers are undoubtedly found and given shelter by other cat lovers, and others picked up as strays en route and put up for adoption in nearby towns and cities. But others, like Swoop, get right to the place they intended to go.

It's the same with us when we embark on a long journey, whether the journey moves us physically from one place to another, or takes us spiritually to new levels of growth and understanding. We know where we'd like to end up, but we have no idea of the twists and turns we might be taking along the way. When the pull is strong enough, however, we'll start out. We'll brave the road ahead, because there's someplace our heart knows we want to go.

*Most of us like to know
what's ahead, yet in so many
of life's important decisions,
we have no such security.
We choose a career. . .say
"I do" at the altar. . .move
to a new city. . .decide to
retire. . .all these journeys
we embark on in the course
of life.*

*A fork in the road. . .an
unexpected detour. . .even
a dead-end along the way
might be part of the journey
and only enriches the route.
Where in your life have you
found this to be true?*

**The most scenic route is
where love and courage
take us.**

No great deed is done by falterers who ask for certainty.
-George Eliot

We are never more in danger than when we think
ourselves most secure, nor in reality more secure than
when we seem to be most in danger.
-William Cowper

Isn't it splendid to think of all the things there are to find
out about? It just makes me feel glad to be alive—it's
such an interesting world. It wouldn't be half so interesting if we knew all about everything, would it? There'd be
no scope for imagination then, would there?
-L. M. Montgomery

All life is an experiment.
The more experiments you make, the better.
-Ralph Waldo Emerson

Great deeds are usually wrought at great risks.
-Herodotus

Uncertainty and expectation are the joys of life.
-William Congreve

# PURRRSONALITY CATS

There are as many cat personalities as there are cats. Like people, each cat possesses a singular attitude and response to the world and relationships…and anyone living under the same roof with several cats knows this by experience.

Our own four cats illustrate the point. The calico is a diva. She's easily irritated and doesn't hesitate to let us know it with what we call her "crabby meow." She sounds forth with her crabby meow when, in her opinion, too much attention is being lavished on one of the other cats…or another cat should happen to cross in front of her line of vision…or she wants up in my lap and I'm slow about making my lap available…or I want to get up before she's ready, and she's obliged to hop down. And she's been known to complain without any obvious provocation.

The tortoiseshell is just as demanding, but of a more easygoing temperament. When she wants up on my lap, she simply jumps up rather than stating her demand from the foot of the chair I'm sitting in. If I need to put her down, she accepts the situation with equanimity, usually finding a nearby spot for the remainder of her nap. When she wants her chin scratched, she holds it out for me to scratch, and responds with purrs and quivering tail— signs of pure bliss.

Our gray tabby cat generally keeps to herself. If she were a person, she'd be the quiet one who would rather watch and listen than participate and be heard. The gray girl has no interest in laps, but she likes to stretch out beside a warm body in bed, and she'll respond to being petted until she gets tired of the attention and simply walks away.

Of our four cats, she's also the most wary. When a visitor enters the door, she'll scamper upstairs until either the visitor leaves, or she deems the person safe enough to encounter, and only then will she venture downstairs and silently creep into the living room.

The white cat is the mild-mannered girl of the household. She likes to take her naps in someone's lap, but if the person makes movements to get up, she gamely jumps down. Most times, she proceeds into the kitchen to see if perhaps the person has gotten up for the purpose of filling her bowl. If not, however, that's OK.

The white cat quietly goes about the business of her day, happily accepting whatever attention comes to her, but being perfectly content to sit by the window and watch birds if nothing else is going on. She rarely raises her voice, believing in the power of action to make her wants known. Planting herself next to the cupboard where her food is kept, for example, gets her point across quite succinctly.

As with a person, you just have to be around a cat for a while before you know the full spectrum of attitudes, habits, and behaviors the cat possesses. Sure, you can get an idea of a cat's temperament with one visit, but it takes time to glimpse the real miracle of an individual personality…a being all its own. And the same can be said about people, too.

Our deeds determine us,
as much as we determine our deeds.
-George Eliot

A humble knowledge of oneself is a surer road to God
than a deep searching of the sciences.
-Thomas à Kempis

Your character is the result of your conduct.
-Aristotle

The Lord seeth not as man seeth;
for man looketh on the outward appearance,
but the Lord looketh on the heart.
-I Samuel 16:7

No man remains quite
what he was when he recognizes himself.
-Thomas Mann

The most difficult thing in life is to know yourself.
-Thales of Miletus

*How much do you know
of your own personality. . .
your unique strengths. . .
your strong points. . .your
weaknesses? What you hear
from others can take you
only so far, because their
perceptions may be colored
by their own judgments and
expectations. A surer way to
learn about your personality
is to look at your actions.*

*The things you do and say
each day give you objective
evidence of the kind of person
you are. Is there a gap
between the person you
think you are and your
daily actions?*

❧

**To know yourself is at the
heart of wisdom.**

You should not live one way in private, another in public.
-Publilus Syrus

No man, for any considerable period, can wear one
face to himself, and another to the multitude, without
finally getting bewildered as to which may be the true.
-Nathaniel Hawthorne

You can tell the character of every man when you see
how he receives praise.
-Seneca

Do not wish to be anything but what you are,
and try to be that perfectly.
-Francis de Sales

Nobody can acquire honor by doing what is wrong.
-Thomas Jefferson

By nothing do men show their character
more than by the things they laugh at.
-Johann von Goethe

# KITTEN ON THE KEYS

———————————•———————————

Where there's a cat and a piano, they will surely come together. At midnight, the cat's humans shoot straight up from sleep to hear an eerie tune emanate from the piano downstairs. A frustrated pianist-turned-burglar? A late-night partier making himself at home in the wrong house? After a few anxious minutes listening to the impromptu concert, the humans breathe a sigh of relief to hear the unmistakable sound of their cat leaping down from the keyboard.

When Ketzel, the black-and-white cat, tried her paws at the grand piano in her home, she captured the attention of her musician-human, who liked the sounds he heard. He quickly transcribed the music, as he had every reason to think this would be a one-time-only performance. Indeed it was.

Now shortly after Ketzel's composition was put on paper, the musician received a notice of a contest for musical compositions under 60 seconds long. He and his wife decided to submit the piece composed by the cat. Though the true identity of the composer was noted, judges were not given this information, but only the music, "Piece for Piano, Four Paws." It received honorable mention, and has been played by several musical ensembles.

The story brings to mind the ragtime piano piece, Kitten on the Keys, by Zez Confrey. Released in 1921 when the composer was playing and editing piano music for a piano roll company, the number became a hit. It was inspired by none other than his grandmother's cat, who liked to trot back and forth along the ivories at regular intervals. Confrey went on to write other novelty pieces for the piano, mini-operas, pop songs, as well as songs for jazz bands.

If we're quick to dismiss the whimsical...the quirky... the things that seemingly don't belong together, we're apt to overlook the essence of creativity and invention. If we have no patience for cats prancing across the ivories, we'll miss the very things that make us smile. If we're too serious for frivolity now and then, we're certainly way too serious!

*Let us be grateful to people who make us happy;*
*they are the charming gardeners*
*who make our souls blossom.*
*-Marcel Proust*

*When was the last time*
*you giggled until tears*
*rolled down your face. . .*
*let yourself follow through*
*on a truly kooky idea. . .*
*kicked back and let your*
*imagination soar?*
*If you can answer*
*"just yesterday"—*
*or better yet, "today"—*
*you're blessed! You're*
*someone who can embrace*
*the humorous and laugh out*
*loud. . .who can connect*
*with creativity (and with*
*others) through the bond*
*of a joyful heart.*

**Let your imagination**
**soar today.**

114

The world is but a canvas to our imaginations.
-Henry David Thoreau

Humor is the only test of gravity,
and gravity of humor; for a subject which will not bear
raillery is suspicious, and a jest which will not bear
serious examination is false wit.
-Aristotle

Creativity is not the finding of a thing,
but the making something out of it after it is found.
-James Russell Lowell

The most manifest sign of wisdom is a
continual cheerfulness; her state is like that in the
regions above the moon, always clear and serene.
-Michel de Montaigne

# VERY SENIOR CATS

As more and more cats become strictly indoor cats, the population of elderly cats continues to climb. Kept safely out of traffic and away from predators, indoor cats are most likely to be spayed or neutered, and receive regular veterinary care. Medicines and treatments for sick cats have become widely available in recent years, and a housecat with 30 or more candles on his catnip birthday cake is not unheard of. By some calculations, a cat of 30 translates to a human of 137!

Stories of cats reaching their 30th birthday and beyond make the rounds of cat magazines and the Internet, although many of the claims cannot be verified for lack of documentation, such as veterinary records, or birth papers in the case of pedigreed animals.

But as with humans, not all seniors owe their longevity to advances in medicines along with a nutritious diet. Granpa Rexs Allen, a Sphynx cat believed to have reached his 34th birthday, enjoyed bacon, eggs, asparagus, mayonnaise, and coffee generously enriched with cream.

Coincidentally, living in the same household as Granpa was Creme Puff, who celebrated her 38th birthday in 2005, and then passed away three days later. She bears the distinction of being the oldest cat with verifiable proof of age, and appears in Guinness World Records, 2010 edition, as the oldest cat known.

Before the advent of modern feline health care, there was Puss, who lived in Devon, England. Puss was reportedly born in 1903 and lived for 36 years, although the date of birth cannot be verified.

These days, Kataleena Lady is a Burmese whose home is or was in Melbourne, Australia. Born in 1977, she is by all accounts still living. If so, she's well into her glorious 30s. No doubt there are many elder cats throughout the world who have passed the quarter-century mark and some even approaching the big 3-0.

People, too, are often blessed with many years, thanks to the advantages of safe and plentiful food, and regular health screenings and examinations. While these things are important, however, they're only the icing on the (birthday) cake, so to speak. We are the handiwork of God, who made us, and our years are given to us from Him as gifts to use, love, and enjoy.

Each year…each day…each hour is a blessing to behold.

*How do you feel when*
*you celebrate "milestone"*
*birthdays? Age jokes and the*
*ribbing that goes with them*
*harp on the negative side*
*of getting older, but there is*
*truly a lot to celebrate with*
*every year. We arrive at*
*each birthday with wisdom*
*we've never had before. . .*
*things we've learned, done,*
*experienced, and achieved.*

*Every year is a milestone,*
*a gift from God to you. . .*
*for you.*

❦

**Every age is the right age**
**to be.**

Each part of life has its own pleasures.
Each has its own abundant harvest, to be garnered in
season. We may grow old in body, but we need never
grow old in mind and spirit.
-Cicero

**The years teach much which the days never knew.**
**-Ralph Waldo Emerson**

In your old age you will complete for the glory of God
the tower of your soul that you began to build in the
golden days of your youth.
-Mother Teresa

**The gradually declining years**
**are among the sweetest in a man's life.**
**-Seneca**

Age is an issue of mind over matter.
If you don't mind, it doesn't matter.
-Mark Twain

# OUR PURRRFECT LOVE

I knew the moment I saw her that she was the one for me. I had gone to the shelter looking for an older cat, and I had my heart set on a calico. I scanned the cats available for adoption, and there she was. My eyes went straight to her, and she immediately stood up from where she had been hunched against the wall and trotted right over to me. I had no doubt but that we were made for each other. With "Yes, I'll take her" and a check written out to the shelter, the calico was now on her way to joining her forever home and family.

The moment she stepped into the house, the comments started rolling in, and they weren't complimentary. Comments like: "Why is she so scruffy looking?" and "She sure is scrawny!" and "Look at her odd markings!" and "Well, she's not a pretty calico, is she?" I was surprised, because I saw her as a beautiful cat with nothing wrong with her that a big helping of her favorite food for a few weeks and a little TLC with the grooming brush wouldn't cure.

As it turned out, I was right about her general health and appearance, and even the naysayers had to admit that she filled out nicely and became, in her own way, an almost-pretty calico cat. But I have found her to be an amazing cat, also. She's loving and loyal, pleasingly possessive and attentively watchful. She has a mind of her own, not caring one whit about where she came from, or her lackluster coat of the past, or what a truly "pretty" calico cat ought to look like. Who decides what "perfect markings" for a calico cat should be, anyway?

The whole incident reminded me that "love is blind" in all the best ways when it simply loves. Love sees beauty in the other, because that's the way love looks at the other. The eyes of love dismiss faults and appreciate what the other has to give without measuring against some other standard.

Love isn't objective, and that's what gives love its mystery, its serendipity, its enchantment, its eternal appeal. "Blind" love gives us a glimpse of how God loves us—not because there's anything "pretty" about us, but because God sees with the eyes of love.

*Love takes many forms, but one of the most mysterious is love at first sight. We lock eyes, and we know there's a special bond between us. It's a feeling of already understanding each other, even though we've yet to exchange names...of belonging together, despite the fact we've barely met.*

*How do you feel about love at first sight...is it reliable? Is it true? Has it ever happened to you?*

❧

**The flower of love can blossom anywhere.**

The conclusion is always the same: love is the most
powerful and still the most unknown energy of the world.
-Teilhard de Chardin

Love is patient, love is kind. It does not envy,
it does not boast, it is not proud. It is not rude,
it is not self-seeking, it is not easily angered,
it keeps no record of wrongs. Love does not delight
in evil but rejoices with the truth. It always protects,
always trusts, always hopes, always perseveres.
-I Corinthians 13:4-7 NIV

A crowd is not company,
faces are but a gallery of pictures,
and talk but a tinkling cymbal,
where there is no love.
-Francis Bacon

It is possible that a man can be so changed by love as
hardly to be recognized as the same person.
-Terence

# THOSE MAGNIFICENT CATS

The cat in your lap is truly an amazing creature! While you stroke her from ears to tail and listen to her purrs of pleasure, consider these facts. She possesses more bones than you do—about 230 to your approximately 206. Although dogs are credited with being able to hear a much wider range of sounds than humans, cats out-hear both dogs and humans. Perhaps that's how she knows to come running when you open the cupboard where her food is kept, even though she's been snoozing three rooms away!

When your cat purrs during her vet's examination, it isn't because she's particularly fond of her doctor or pleased to be poked and prodded with sundry syringes and instruments. While purrs certainly signal pleasure under the right conditions, her distinctive rumble can also mean she's scared silly, or at least sufficiently nervous to let you know how she feels. Purring is like someone responding to what you have said with "Well…" The meaning of that single word "well" depends on where it comes in the conversation and the tone of voice in which it's uttered.

Your cat's occasional spells of bewildering behavior, marked by tearing through the house at breakneck speeds (possibly as fast as 30 mph), is her way of using up excess energy. She's making up for the fact she doesn't need to chase her meals through dense forests before she can eat.

And these might sound like low numbers to you if brushing cat hair off of your clothing and furniture is a daily task, but there are approximately 60,000 hairs per square inch on your cat's back and about 120,000 per square inch on her underside. How many square inches span your cat's back and her underside, and then how many hairs encompass your cat, might be something for you and a mathematically inclined friend to figure out together sometime.

Yes, your cat is a magnificent creature…almost as magnificent as you are. You're the one who picked her out from all the others…who opened your door to let her in. You shelter her, provide for her, and love her. She depends on you every day of her life.

You are using the resources and abilities your heavenly Father has given you to care for another living being—and that's a truly magnificent thing to do.

*We reflect God's love for*
*us when we care for and*
*about others. Those who*
*depend on us for support,*
*encouragement, or friendship*
*are the gifts God gives so we*
*can know the satisfaction*
*of helping and providing*
*for others.*

*People, animals, and all*
*God's creation invite us to*
*give of ourselves. . .to work*
*for the good. . .to shower*
*His blessings over all.*
*How does what you do*
*for others reflect God's*
*goodness to you?*

❧

**An ounce of help is better**
**than a pound of pity.**

I will praise thee; for I am fearfully
and wonderfully made: marvelous are thy works.
-Psalm 139:14


Every man is the builder of the temple
called his body—we are all sculptors and painters,
and our material is our flesh and blood and bones.
Any nobleness begins at once to refine a man's features.
-Henry David Thoreau


What do we live for, if not to
make life less difficult for each other?
-George Eliot


God made the human body,
and it is the most exquisite and wonderful organization
which has come to us from the divine hand.
-Henry Ward Beecher


Everything that lives, lives not alone, nor for itself.
-William Blake


She gives most who gives with joy.
-Mother Teresa

# THE RESCUED CAT

Jennifer, a college student, walked across the quad one afternoon and saw about six or seven boys gathered around something they were poking with their feet and then guffawing loudly. "Adolescent idiots," she muttered, and just as she was about to look the other way, she realized the "thing" they were kicking was alive. The little creature was scampering this way and that way in a pitiful attempt to escape the circle of shoes and boots tormenting it.

Alarmed, Jennifer ran over to the huddle. "Hey, what are you doing?" she shouted, and the distress in her voice caught the attention of several other students in the quad. Within seconds, a small group of people had gathered behind the girl. The boys immediately stopped what they were doing, a couple with embarrassed looks on their faces, and others adopting a devil-may-care swagger as they faced Jennifer and the curious stares of their fellow students.

"That poor kitten!" Jennifer exclaimed when she saw the trembling animal. Before she could bend down to pick it up, however, it ran into nearby bushes, out of reach and out of sight. Jennifer felt anger rising from her stomach to her cheeks, and she knew they had turned flaming red. "How could you? How could you do that to a poor defenseless kitten?" she screamed.

The couple of head-hanging boys scanned the pavement for an answer, while the one who had been doing most of the guffawing spoke for the group. "Oh, loosen up," he said with an indolent drawl. "We weren't doing anything to hurt it. We were just havin' a little fun."

"How is kicking a tiny creature, by any definition, considered fun?" she demanded, angrier yet because of the boy's attitude. "Aw, come on," the lead boy drawled. With an expletive, he jerked his head to his pals. "Let's get out of here, guys." And with that, they sauntered off, a few with sloped shoulders and the rest maintaining their swagger.

"I wonder where it went?" asked one of the onlookers, a senior girl carrying her backpack and a stack of library books. She put her things on a bench and proceeded to probe the bushes while softly calling the kitten. Just as Jennifer was about to follow the senior girl in search of the kitten, she felt a gentle hand on her shoulder.

"Hey, that was awful what happened." She quickly turned and found herself staring into the bluest eyes she had ever seen. "I really admire what you did," he added, his face visibly softening as he focused on her face. He saw intelligent eyes still passionate with feeling, a nose bridged with a smattering of sun-kissed freckles, ruddy cheeks, and soft, expressive lips, all framed by long, full chestnut hair.

As naturally pretty as Jennifer was, she was the kind of girl boys often overlooked. First, she was a serious girl, determined to finish college and go on to grad school. Second, she shunned makeup and tattoos, along with sassy, revealing clothes. Third, she was really shy around boys, and when they tried to talk to her, she froze, mumbling something incoherent that effectively ended the conversation. But now her mind was on the kitten, and the boy's sincere concern touched her.

"I've got him!" called one of the students who had gone looking for the cat, and her shout immediately got Jennifer and the boy's attention. The girl, cuddling the little bundle of gray in her arms, was joined by everyone else. Together, the students formed a circle of love and affection, oohing and aaahing over the kitten they had rescued from its tormentors. Jennifer held out her arms as the girl carefully transferred the kitten to her.

"Oh, what a darling baby!" she cooed, as the boy scratched the creature's ears. "I'll take you home, OK?" The kitten seemed to pick up on the goodness showered upon it, because Jennifer felt its fragile body relax in her arms and noticed its big round eyes no longer radiated fear.

Jennifer thanked everyone who had helped, and she skipped her afternoon American history class to take the kitten back to her apartment. But not before the boy with the blue eyes introduced himself as Brian and asked if she'd be interested in going out for pizza that evening.

She flashed a bashful smile, a smile that still could melt his heart. At their 20th anniversary celebration, they posed for a photo—a handsome couple surrounded by two vibrant teen girls and one athletic blue-eyed boy. Comfortably seated in the middle was a large gray cat looking pleased as could be, surrounded by the loves of his life.

"Things turned out well for him," I said to a college friend who had witnessed the incident with me.

"Yes," she said, "things sure did. And turned out pretty well for them, too," she added, and raised a glass to the happy family.

*We might feel afraid to
confront bullies head-on.
Perhaps they will turn
on us, or ridicule us, or
retaliate in some way.
Our fear, however, allows
meanness to continue, more
and more certain of its
power to intimidate and
terrify us.*

*Have you ever been called
upon to intervene
in a bad situation?
What happened?*

**Do all the good you can,
at all the times you can.**

The coward only threatens when he is safe.
-Johann Von Goethe

In difficult situations, when hope seems feeble,
the boldest plans are safest.
-Livy

Attacking is the only secret.
Dare and the world always yields; or if it beats you
sometimes, dare it again, and it will succumb.
-William Makepeace Thackeray

No man chooses evil because it is evil;
he only mistakes it for happiness, the good he seeks.
-Mary Wollstonecraft

Do not withhold good from those who deserve it,
when it is in your power to act.
-Proverbs 3:27 NIV

The best portion of a good man's life is his little,
nameless, unremembered acts of kindness and of love.
-William Wordsworth

# HERDING CATS

I love my cats, yet from time to time I toy with the idea of adding a dog to the household. A dog would be a companion for me when I walk, and might even get me walking more regularly than I do. But a couple times every day, like my neighbor does? In good weather or bad, she's out there walking Maggie while I'm inside, cozy in the winter and cool in the summer, with my equally comfortable cats.

In favor of a dog, though, is the story a neighbor told me not too long ago. During the night, burglars attempted to break into her house, but just as they were jimmying open a window, their beagle barked and woke them up and sent the would-be burglars scampering the other way. I'm not sure what my cats would do in such a situation, but I fear it might be what I would do: hide.

So if I wake up around one or two in the morning and think I hear a noise downstairs, a barking, howling, ferocious-sounding dog seems like just the ticket. But then when daylight floods the room and I get up to plug in the coffee, I look out my kitchen window to see another neighbor who's bundled in her bathrobe, standing on the driveway while her Dalmatian does his duty. I wonder if there's such a thing as a litter box for dogs.

But the number-one trait about cats that makes me think I ought to stick with them completely is their independence. Devoted dog owners, when they plan to be gone all day, will bring the dog with them, if they can...or drop him off at doggy daycare...or have someone come at noon to see to his needs... or come home early. With a household of cats, all I need to do is make sure their bowls are filled and their water fresh and their litter boxes clean, and I'm gone for the rest of the day. I don't worry about them, because I know exactly what they're doing (sleeping), and I know they won't miss me until it's time to go to bed. When I come home unusually late, they will be waiting for me at the door, perhaps concerned about those food bowls; otherwise, my comings and goings are of little concern to them.

Their self-sufficiency is admirable, except, of course, when I want to get them to do something, like come out of hiding, or play with toys I just spent a small fortune to buy, or sit on my lap, or get themselves off today's crossword puzzle. Then I understand why the phrase "it's like herding cats" describes something frustratingly difficult, if not impossible.

Cats like to do what we like to do, and that's go our own way. When something attracts us, we want to saunter over and take a look at it. When we don't feel like doing something, we're not likely to do it…or if we do, our heart and mind drift elsewhere for the duration. It takes practice and self-discipline not to let our "cat-like" nature lure us off the path God has laid out for us. No, He won't herd us…He's given us a will all our own. But He is always ready and willing to gently guide us along the way He would invite us to go.

The fruit of the Spirit is love, joy, peace,
patience, kindness, goodness, faithfulness,
gentleness and self-control.
-Galatians 5:22-23 NIV

I count him braver who overcomes his desires
than him who conquers his enemies;
for the hardest victory is over self.
-Aristotle

Let everyone who has the grace of
intelligence fear that, because of it, he will be judged
more heavily if he is negligent.
-Bridget of Sweden

Not being able to govern events,
I govern myself, and apply myself to them,
if they will not apply themselves to me.
-Michel de Montaigne

Hold yourself responsible for a higher standard than
anybody else expects of you. Never excuse yourself.
Never pity yourself. Be a hard master to yourself—
and be lenient to everybody else.
-Henry Ward Beecher

*Much has been made of
the difference between "cat
people" and "dog people."
Why do you think cats or
dogs may match certain
personalities? Yet how many
examples can you think
of that belie commonly
accepted differences?*

*Though they each have
their own traits and
characteristics, needs and
requirements, both cats and
dogs bless the lives of those
who love them!*

❧

**God has given you
everything you need to
follow your path of life.**

I am, indeed, a king, because I know how to rule myself.
-Pietro Aretino

I long to put the experience of fifty years at once into
your young lives, to give you at once the key to that
treasure chamber, every gem of which has cost me tears
and struggles and prayers, but you must work for these
inward treasures yourselves.
-Harriet Beecher Stowe

Nothing gives one person so much advantage
over another as to remain always cool
and unruffled under all circumstances.
-Thomas Jefferson

There is no allurement or enticement,
actual or imaginary, which a well-disciplined mind may
not surmount. The wish to resist more than
half accomplishes the object.
-Charlotte Dacre

It is not enough to have great qualities;
we should also have the management of them.
-François de La Rochefoucauld

# THE CAT AND THE VACUUM

I t's the vacuum cleaner that worries Sally's cat, Feathers. Sally believes that Feathers' fear of the vacuum began the day Sally pushed the roaring machine into a walk-in closet where, unknown to her, Feathers was sleeping. The next thing she knew, a black cat with her long fur standing on end and saucer-sized eyes blazing zoomed passed her, out the closet, and disappeared.

Several hours of vacuum-free silence reigned over the house before Feathers cautiously emerged from her hiding place. The cat stuck close to the walls, eyeing available means of escape, until she assured herself the vacuum was safely contained.

Now, years later, Feathers goes into hiding whenever Sally brings out the vacuum—the cat doesn't even wait for her to turn it on. Even if Sally's cleaning takes her nowhere near the cat's current resting spot, Feathers takes cover someplace out of sight.

Many times, however, where Feathers chooses to hide is right where Sally intends to vacuum, and so begins Feathers' run from room to room, each time followed in several minutes by Sally and the fearsome beast.

"She gets more and more agitated," Sally reported. "I wish I could tell her that the walk-in closet 'attack' was a mistake—it won't happen again!" But according to Feathers, it could…and she doesn't want to be around if it does.

When I think of Feathers and her fear of the vacuum, it reminds me of times I'm afraid to attempt something because I tried it once, and it failed…or backfired…or flopped completely. Rather than look at the specific circumstances and examine what I did and what I could do differently, I decide—like Feathers—to distance myself from the whole thing. Just not go there.

I have to remind myself that one bad encounter doesn't mean I had a run-in with a malicious beast out to get me. It just means I've learned a lesson…and that's a good thing. When I go for it again, perhaps the "beast" won't look so beastly after all…or maybe might be afraid of me!

*We should be careful to get out of an experience only the wisdom that is in it and stop there, lest we be like the cat that sits down on a hot stove-lid. She will never sit down on a hot stove-lid again, and that is well; but also she will never sit down on a cold one anymore.*
*-Mark Twain*

*"I'll never do that again!"*
*Sometimes those are wise*
*words—the plan was*
*ill-advised in the first place,*
*and we learned the hard*
*way why it was not a good*
*idea. But when the plan was*
*a good one and we didn't*
*succeed with it, those same*
*words could be the ending*
*of something still open and*
*leading to a very good place.*
*What valuable lessons have*
*you learned from your*
*mistakes?*

❧

**A mistake is evidence that**
**you have experience...**
**and experience brings**
**wisdom.**

I have learned more from my mistakes
than from my successes.
-Humphry Davy

Apparent failure may hold in its rough shell
the germs of a success that will blossom in time,
and bear fruit throughout eternity.
-Frances Ellen Watkins Harper

We may make mistakes—
but they must never be mistakes which result from
faintness of heart or abandonment of moral principle.
-Franklin D. Roosevelt

Failure after long perseverance
is much grander than never to have a striving good
enough to be called a failure.
-George Eliot

No man ever became great or good
except through many and great mistakes.
-William Gladstone

A kitten is the most irresistible comedian in the world. Its wide-open eyes gleam with wonder and mirth. It darts madly at nothing at all, and then, as though suddenly checked in the pursuit, prances sideways on its hind legs with ridiculous agility and zeal.

-Agnes Repplier